# Skating Superstars

Written by
## Debbi Wilkes

Photographs by
## Gérard Châtaigneau

**Scholastic Canada Ltd.**
Toronto  New York  London  Auckland  Sydney
Mexico City  New Delhi  Hong Kong  Buenos Aires

# Irina Slutskaya

Born: February 9, 1979
In: Moscow, Russia
Home: Moscow, Russia
Height: 160 cm (5'3")
Coach: Zhanna Gromova
Trains in: Moscow
Choreographers: Viacheslav Voituk, Igor Bobrin
Category: Ladies' singles
Representing: Russia

She's been called The Comeback Kid.

Despite her many wins, Irina Slutskaya was pretty much given up for lost a year ago. Since winning her first world title in 2002, she'd suffered through illnesses, injuries and setbacks, including heart problems and worry over her mother's near-fatal kidney condition. Finally the bottom fell out at the 2004 World Championships when Irina finished ninth — totally out of the medals.

The skating world had written her off. Yet Irina felt that no one else should decide whether she could still compete. She refused to listen to any negative thoughts about her skating future. Instead she listened to her doctors.

Taking it carefully, Irina began training again in Moscow. As she got back into shape, she uncovered her competitive spark. With her lifetime coach, Zhanna Gromova, by her side, and with the support of her husband, Sergei Mikheyev, Irina was back on track.

Right from the very beginning of the 2004–2005 season, Irina took control of her skating. She performed with her trademark fresh-faced, natural style —

only this time she also tapped into a new kind of confidence and joy, attacking each program with passion.

Irina won every event she entered! Cup of China, Cup of Russia, the Grand Prix Final . . . and the jewel in the crown, the world championships. Suddenly the underdog was a favorite once again.

Irina's list of firsts is unmatched: first Russian woman to win the European title and Olympic silver; first woman to land a triple-Lutz triple-loop combination in competition; first woman to land two triple-triple combinations in the same program; first woman to land a triple-Lutz triple-loop double-toe combination. The Russians have never before had a Ladies' competitor with Irina's skills, star quality and staying power.

Irina has climbed back to the top. Now there's just one thing missing from her list of firsts: first Russian woman to be crowned Olympic figure skating champion.

## Highlights

1st at World Championships 2005, 2002

1st at European Championships 2005, 2003, 2001, 2000, 1997, 1996

1st at Russian National Championships 2005, 2002, 2001, 2000

1st at Grand Prix Final 2005, 2002

2nd at Olympic Games 2002

2nd at World Championships 2001, 2000, 1998

2nd at European Championships 1998

2nd at Russian National Championships 1996

3rd at World Championships 1996

# Jeffrey Buttle

Born: September 1, 1982
In: Smooth Rock Falls, Ontario
Home: Barrie, Ontario
Height: 173 cm (5'8")
Coaches: Lee Barkell, Rafael Aratunian
Trains in: Barrie, Ontario / Lake Arrowhead, California
Choreographer: David Wilson
Category: Men's singles
Representing: Canada

To some skating fans, Jeffrey Buttle was a surprise medalist at the 2005 World Championships in Moscow, but back home in Canada, his win was a thrilling tribute to an emerging champion.

Jeffrey's love of skating began at the age of two. Ten years later he was still unable to do even one triple jump, until joining the famous Mariposa Skating School under coach Lee Barkell. Within one year he'd learned every triple jump except the axel. Since then he has mastered the triple axel and the quadruple toe loop. Jeffrey's slight body size — perfect for a skater — helps him spin fast and control his jumps more easily. But the focus of his skating today is on his choreography.

Choreographer David Wilson — a man Jeffrey calls a genius — helps him to "hear the story" of the music and use the rhythms to improve his jumps and spins. Every note is important, and if Jeffrey doesn't concentrate on his music, he tends to worry too much about his jumps.

Jeffrey loves understanding how things work — he's a chemical engineering student at university. For the moment, though, he's put his education on hold to concentrate on his training — some of it in California, where he works alongside Michelle Kwan and her coach Rafael Aratunian. It's an inspiring environment that gives Jeffrey the opportunity to witness first-hand Michelle's incredible work habits and her constant dedication — factors both athletes share.

When Jeffrey suffered a serious bout of food poisoning days before the 2003–2004 Grand Prix Final and was hospitalized, losing seven pounds almost overnight, it was a huge setback. He never recovered his strength that season and was devastated not to make the team heading to the world championships. But within days of that result, Jeffrey's determination kicked back in and he starting working harder than ever. Less than a year later, his hard work paid off when he skated away with the 2005 Canadian title. That win gave him so much confidence that he repeated his inspired performance at the world championships to win the silver medal for Canada.

## Highlights

1st at Canadian National Championships 2005

1st at Four Continents 2002

1st at NHK Trophy 2003

1st at Cup of China 2004

2nd at World Championships 2005

2nd at Grand Prix Final 2004

# Belbin ★ Agosto

Born: July 11, 1984 / January 15, 1982
In: Kingston, Ontario / Chicago, Illinois
Home: Bloomfield Hills, Michigan
Height: 167 cm (5'6") / 175 cm (5'9")
Coaches: Igor Shpilband, Marina Zoueva
Train in: Canton, Michigan
Choreographer: Igor Shpilband
Category: Dance
Representing: USA

*T*anith Belbin and Ben Agosto are the first U.S. ice dancers to win a world medal in twenty years.

Tanith grew up in Kirkland, Quebec, and began skating at the age of two because her mom, Michelle, was a skating coach. In her early competitive days, Tanith studied pairs skating as well as dancing, using pairs training to strengthen her general skating ability. These days she confesses to being a bit of a daredevil, especially when she's busy with one of her favorite hobbies, car racing.

When Ben's not on the ice, he unwinds by playing electric guitar and piano — or, when he's in an adventuresome mood, by rock climbing or dodging blasts from his friends' paintball guns.

It was 1998 when Ben moved to Detroit from his home in Chicago to team up with Tanith and train under the expert eye of Russian coaches Igor Shpilband and Marina Zoueva.

The team is a fascinating combination of movie-star good looks and athleticism. They have a distinctive talent for interpreting a wide variety of music. Unlike so many Russian-coached skaters, Tanith and Ben's style is understated and clean, relying on their top-notch skating skills rather than on overly dramatic presentation. They won the world junior title in 2002 and followed it with a meteoric rise, winning their first U.S. national senior title in 2004.

The pair's long-term goal is to become the first U.S. ice dancing team to win the world championships and eventually the Olympic Games. For the world event, Tanith and Ben are right on target. But without a bit of a miracle — regardless of their success — the couple will not be on the U.S. Olympic team for 2006. Although Tanith has applied for her American citizenship, she may not receive it until long after the Olympic flame is doused in Turin, Italy.

"That's OK," says Tanith. "Ben and I are here for the long haul . . . and Vancouver in 2010 gives us four more years to get that much better!"

## Highlights

1st at US National Championships 2005, 2004

1st at Four Continents 2005

1st at World Junior Championships 2002

2nd at World Championships 2005

2nd at Grand Prix Final 2005

2nd at World Junior Championships 2001

5th at World Championships 2004

# Sasha Cohen

Born: October 26, 1984

In: Westwood, California

Home: Laguna Niguel, California

Height: 157 cm (5'2")

Coach: John Nicks

Trains in: Aliso Viejo, California

Choreographer: Nikolai Morozov

Category: Ladies' singles

Representing: USA

At the Opening Ceremonies of the 2002 Olympic Games, an American figure skater sat in the bleachers, talking on her cell phone to the President of the United States and asking him if he'd mind saying a few words to her mother.

That young Olympian, Alexandra Pauline "Sasha" Cohen, never actually wanted to be a skater. Gymnastics was her thing, but when she was injured at an early age, her mom, Galina, switched her talented seven-year-old to skating.

From the start of Sasha's competitive career, it wasn't her jumps or spins that got her noticed. It was her on-ice presence, her flexibility and her flair for the dramatic. Sasha was trying all the big tricks too, although with her wild jumps, she spent much of her time sprawled on the ice.

Enter coach John Nicks.

Nicks saw something promising and exciting in Sasha and set to work to groom her for the difficult years ahead. After several seasons of up-and-down results, Sasha wowed the crowd at U.S. nationals, finishing a remarkable second. Fans love her ability to do the "Charlotte" — a backward spiral in full split position — a feature that shows her incredible flexibility and has become one of her signature moves.

With Sasha's enormous star power, she has that magical ability to hold an audience in the palm of her hand. To hold the attention of Olympic judges, however, she'll also need consistent jumps. Nicks encourages Sasha to express the emotion of her music, as long as it doesn't take her focus off how important it is to land her jumps.

Sasha has written her autobiography, *Fire On Ice*, in which fans can get to know the champion even better . . . including meeting her cats Mia and Meow and her dog Mocha! And she has appeared in the high-fashion French *V* magazine, *Seventeen* magazine and *Vogue* — all thrilling opportunities for someone who helps design her own costumes and is bent on a career in fashion.

If two world silver medals have given Sasha the confidence to put emotional performances and solid jumps on the ice at the same time, get ready for fireworks!

## Highlights

1st at Skate Canada 2003, 2002

1st at Trophée Lalique 2003

2nd at World Championships 2005, 2004

2nd at US National Championships 2005, 2004, 2002, 2000

2nd at Grand Prix Final 2004

4th at Olympic Games 2002

# Brian Joubert

Born: September 20, 1984
In: Poitiers, France
Home: Poitiers, France
Height: 179 cm (5'10½")
Coach: Andreï Berezintsev
Trains in: Poitiers, France
Choreographer: Nikolai Morozov
Category: Men's singles
Representing: France

Brian Joubert first stepped onto the ice when he was four. Hockey was his first choice, but when his mom put him in skating lessons, he quickly discovered the thrill of jumping . . . and just as quickly decided to forget about hockey.

Brian's talent for turning in the air was so natural, the jumps all came easily to him. By the time he was fifteen, he was already landing the quad toe. These days his focus has expanded beyond the number and quality of his jumps. In today's competitions, judges are looking for much more than how many times you can turn in the air.

A few years ago, Veronique Guyon, then Brian's long-term coach, could see what her skater was lacking. She encouraged him to work with new people, including Laurent Depouilly and Tatiana Tarasova, the great Russian coach then working in America. (Her famous student, Olympic champion Alexei Yagudin, is Brian's idol.)

On trips to the U.S. to work with Tarasova, the team would work almost all night at the rink to push Brian's ability. By stretching his body into new positions and his mind into new ideas, the plan was to reshape him into the "total package" needed today. He already had great jumps and the perfect look — handsome face, sparkling eyes, brilliant smile and muscular body. Now they had to bring out his emotion.

After winning the world silver medal in 2004, Brian expected to be back near the top the next year, and well on his way to an Olympic medal. But the skating gods didn't agree. At the next world championships, Brian fell off the medal podium — all the way down to sixth. But his dedicated fans (who call him "Baboo," a childhood nickname) expect his triumphant return for the Olympic Games. After all, anyone who's worked with Brian talks about his fighting spirit and perseverance.

Brian says it all: "I want to win!" Whether he's training on the ice, relaxing with his friends or at home playing with his English bulldog, Blade, Brian's sights are clearly set on Olympic glory.

## Highlights

1st at European Championships 2004

1st at French National Championships 2005, 2004, 2003

1st at Skate America 2004

2nd at World Championships 2004

2nd at European Championships 2005, 2003

6th at World Championships 2005

# Navka ★ Kostomarov

Born: April 13, 1975 / February 8, 1977

In: Dnepropetrovsk, Ukraine / Moscow, Russia

Home: Moscow, Russia

Height: 170 cm (5'7") / 183 cm (6')

Coach: Alexander Zhulin

Train in: Montclair, New Jersey

Choreographers: Tatiana Druchinina, Alexander Zhulin

Category: Dance

Representing: Russia

No one would argue that with two world championship titles, Russians Tatiana Navka and Roman Kostomarov are definitely the favorites to become the 2006 Olympic ice dancing champions. It sounds like the set-up to the perfect success story, but if you look more closely, you'll discover that the story almost didn't get past the first chapter.

Back in the mid 1990s, both skaters had been competing with other partners, Tatiana even representing another country. In 1998 Tatiana and Roman decided to team up with each other for the first time, but the partnership, with only limited success, lasted just one season. Roman formed a new duo with another dancer, and Tatiana retired from competition.

Although Tatiana's competitive spark was still alive, her life was moving in other directions too. In 2000, with the birth of her daughter, Alexandra, she had started enjoying family life away from the rink . . . until the phone rang.

It was Roman, begging Tatiana to start over. Just twelve days after giving birth, she was back skating with Roman, training harder than ever. This time, though, they kept their coaching close to home under the guidance of Tatiana's husband, Alexander Zhulin, a former world ice dancing champion. (Tatiana still remembers the first day she met Alexander — she was just seven when he performed in her home town and she got his autograph.)

Coach Zhulin believes in the incredible potential of his team, and designs programs to showcase their deep edges and their incredible speed and flow. And their height allows both skaters to emphasize their long and graceful body lines.

What other plans do they have to help them along the path to Olympic gold? They believe in the high quality of their skating and have choreographed new programs jammed with difficult elements, such as complicated lifts and intricate footwork. To launch themselves even further above their competitors, they also want to create inventive programs and to skate them with a style that is unique, something the sports world will never forget. Something worthy of Olympic champions.

## Highlights

1st at World Championships 2005, 2004

1st at European Championships 2005, 2004

1st at Russian National Championships 2004, 2003

1st at Grand Prix Final 2005, 2004

10th at Olympic Games 2002

# Carolina Kostner

Born: February 8, 1987
In: Bolzano, Italy
Home: Ortisei, Italy
Height: 168 cm (5'6")
Coach: Michael Huth
Trains in: Oberstdorf, Germany
Choreographers: Megan Smith, Kurt Browning
Category: Ladies' singles
Representing: Italy

*L*ook at Carolina Kostner's family history and you begin to understand one reason why her skating is ranked so high — third in the world. Her mother, Patrizia, was a nationally ranked figure skater. Her father, Erwin, played Olympic and world-level hockey for the Italian national team. And she's the cousin and godchild of Italian skier Isolde Kostner.

Italy couldn't be happier with Carolina's results. With the 2006 Winter Olympics being held in Turin, Italy, Carolina's country is hoping that more medals are in the future for this shy teenager from Ortisei.

Since the age of four, Carolina has been in the skating rink or on the ski slopes. She was twelve when she made the decision to concentrate on skating and perfecting her triple jumps. Everything was going smoothly until several years ago, when a landslide destroyed her training rink. She was forced to find a new training base in Oberstdorf, Germany, where Michael Huth is her coach. Each summer she also spends time in Canada at the Royal Glenora Club in Edmonton, to work on her choreography with former world champion Kurt Browning.

During the competitive season, Carolina finds that life gets very complicated — like many athletes, she struggles to keep up with her education while she's on the road. Traveling to so many other countries has certainly helped with her language studies, though. She speaks five languages: Italian, German, French, English and Ladinic (an Italian dialect), and hopes that some day she'll be able to use them in her career.

One of the things that sets Carolina apart is her tremendous speed. She gallops across the ice to make her jumps bigger. It's a strategy that usually works for her jumps, but it makes it harder for her to control other details, such as arm positions and leg extensions.

As the Olympics draw nearer, Carolina is aware of the expectations from her country. Though she is Italy's big medal hope in figure skating and is excited by the attention, she's determined it will not change her — she skates not for fame but because she loves it!

## Highlights

1st at Italian National Championships 2005, 2003

2nd at Italian National Championships 2004

3rd at World Championships 2005

3rd at World Junior Championships 2003

4th at European Championships 2003

5th at European Championships 2004

7th at European Championships 2005

10th at World Championships 2003

# Stéphane Lambiel

Born: April 2, 1985

In: Martigny, Switzerland

Home: Saxon, Switzerland

Height: 176 cm (5'9")

Coaches: Peter Grütter, Cédric Monod

Trains in: Geneva and Lausanne, Switzerland

Choreographer: Salomé Brunner

Category: Men's singles

Representing: Switzerland

*P*rior to becoming a world champion, Stéphane Lambiel had growing pains just like every other teenager. But shortly after graduating from high school, he was training hard for the upcoming season when he injured his knee so badly he had to have surgery, which kept him off the ice and out of competition for months.

During his recovery, Stéphane spent a lot of time thinking about his career and where his life was going. He'd never lived away from his small home town in Saxon, and for nine years one man, coach Peter Grütter, had directed his skating. Grütter was also a father figure to Stéphane, guiding more than just his steps on the ice.

In time, a feeling that he needed more freedom bothered Stéphane. He abruptly decided to part ways with his coach, fire his management team and split up with his girlfriend.

Suddenly he was on his own. He moved away to the bustling city of Lausanne, enrolled in Economics at university and, when his knee healed, started the search for a new coach.

In the short term, coach Cédric Monod gave Stéphane full support as he worked to regain his balance. It wasn't long, however, before Stéphane realized he still needed Grütter's expertise. In an emotional reunion, the two joined forces once again to prepare for the 2005 European and World Championships. Only this time Coach Grütter was teaching an even more upbeat and determined skater than before.

After Europeans they began work on a brand new free skate to the soundtrack of the movie *King Arthur*. Like most Swiss skaters, Stéphane can spin like a top, but it was the power of the new music that allowed him to regain his triple and quad jumps, and the music's emotion that inspired his fresh creativity.

The combination proved unbeatable. At the 2005 World Championships, with two quad jumps in his free skate, Stéphane became the first men's world champion from Switzerland in nearly sixty years . . . and only the third Swiss world champion in the history of skating.

## Highlights

1st at World Championships 2005

1st at Swiss National Championships 2005, 2004, 2003, 2002, 2001

4th at European Championships 2005

4th at World Championships 2004

10th at World Championships 2003

# Michelle Kwan

Born: July 7, 1980

In: Torrance, California

Home: Manhattan Beach, California

Height: 158 cm (5'2")

Coach: Rafael Aratunian

Trains in: Lake Arrowhead, California

Choreographer: Nikolai Morozov

Category: Ladies' singles

Representing: USA

No figure skater in modern times is more decorated and celebrated than American Michelle Kwan.

It's partly her elegance and class, and partly her high level of talent, training and concentration that make Michelle such a legend. She has won more than forty major championships — in the process receiving more than fifty perfect marks of 6.0!

Michelle credits her love of skating to her parents, Estella and Danny, who always taught her that, win or lose, if she worked hard and tried her best, there was never anything to be ashamed of. And she did work hard.

At five she was trying on her first pair of skates. By thirteen she was an up-and-comer, sitting in the stands at the 1994 Olympic Games in Norway, getting her first taste of high-level international competition. Just two years later, she had climbed to the top of the podium as world champion, a feat she has repeated four more times.

In a sport that can twist your fate in a nanosecond, Michelle doesn't rely on luck (despite the fact that she wears her grandmother's good luck charm around her neck). What has made her a champion is her mental toughness: her ability to react well to unexpected events and to navigate the many other bumps along the way.

Michelle is always looking for new ways to express herself. She does this mostly through her music — anything from classical to pop, each selection chosen for its elegance and beauty. Each program features her trademark change-of-edge spiral. Although Michelle's technical elements have not changed much over time, no skater performs with more passion.

Michelle is a spokesperson for the Children's Miracle Network, was named one of *People* magazine's 50 Most Beautiful People, and created a U.S. scholarship program for female college athletes. She even has her own interactive video game! Her fans — called Kwan-atics — who search the Web for her name will find hundreds of thousands of pages of information, everything from her birth date, to what she studied at university, to who designed her latest costume.

What the Web can't tell us is whether Michelle Kwan will fulfill her life-long dream of becoming the next Olympic champion.

## Highlights

1st at World Championships 2003, 2001, 2000, 1998, 1996

1st at US National Championships 2005, 2004, 2003, 2002, 2001, 2000, 1999, 1998, 1996

2nd at Olympic Games 1998

3rd at Olympic Games 2002

3rd at World Championships 2004

4th at World Championships 2005

# Pang ★ Tong

Born: December 24, 1979 / August 15, 1979
In: Harbin, China
Home: Harbin, China
Height: 162 cm (5'4") / 180 cm (5'11")
Coach: Bin Yao
Train in: Beijing, China
Choreographer: Alexander Zhulin
Category: Pairs
Representing: China

**P**airs skating in China began because of one man: Bin Yao, the country's first pairs skater. Along with his partner, Bo Luan, he never even came close to winning a world event. In fact, the team placed last at the 1980 World Championships, attempting lifts that they'd taught themselves from pictures in a book.

Since then, Bin Yao has studied pairs skating so well, he's become China's national coach and has made the country a major pairs-skating power. He's the engine in a well-oiled machine that boasts three teams ranked among the top five in the world.

One of those teams is Qing Pang and Jian Tong, two young skaters from Harbin, in the northeastern part of China.

Both had learned to skate when they were six, Qing at the outdoor rink at her school and Jian as a roller skater. Over time, as their love for skating grew, they began to compete in singles events. Qing remembers landing her first triple Salchow when she was eight. Jian didn't like jumps as much and switched to ice dancing for a couple of years — where he developed his

beautiful posture and presentation.

Yao put them together in 1993, then suddenly was named national coach and moved to Beijing, leaving Qing and Jian to work on their own.

By watching videos and exchanging ideas with other skaters, Qing and Jian found their own way of doing things, and their own style. It was hard being without a coach. But instead of relying on someone else to solve their problems, they depended on each other.

After four years of separation, they were finally reunited with Yao, who then added some finishing touches to the waif-like Qing and the graceful Jian, by working to improve their strength and musicality.

The pair is considered a long shot for the 2006 Olympic title, but since they're one of the few teams in the world capable of landing a throw quadruple jump, their technical ability could become a deciding factor in the race for Olympic gold.

## Highlights

1st at Four Continents 2004, 2002

1st at Chinese National Championships 2004, 2000

2nd at Four Continents 2005, 2003

3rd at World Championships 2004

4th at World Championships 2005, 2003

9th at Olympic Games 2002

# Evan Lysacek

Born: June 4, 1985
In: Chicago, Illinois
Home: Naperville, Illinois
Height: 180 cm (5'11")
Coaches: Frank Carroll, Ken Congemi
Trains in: El Segundo, California
Choreographer: Oleg Epstein
Category: Men's singles
Representing: USA

Most skaters assume that in their first appearance at a world championship, they'll compete for the international experience rather than for the medals. Evan Lysacek was one of those skaters, thrilled with being named to the world team. No one was more surprised than Evan when he mounted the podium at the 2005 Worlds in Moscow — his very first senior world competition — to receive a bronze medal.

As an eight-year-old hockey wannabe, Evan had never seriously considered taking skating lessons until his grandmother bought him skates for Christmas. He thought group lessons might help improve his hockey skills, but once he started jumping and spinning, he knew he had to change sports. Since then, he's never looked back, starting his competitive wins at the ripe old age of eleven, when he won the Junior Olympics at the juvenile level.

Most of his training has allowed Evan to remain close to home and to his two sisters, but in 2003 he moved to California to be coached by Frank Carroll. It didn't take Carroll long to realize that his new student was a tremendous athlete, with natural jumping ability, but he needed more than jumps to be successful. With time and trust, Carroll was able to encourage Evan to try new things artistically — to be more daring when he was on the ice. With Carroll's legendary skill at building a skater's confidence, Evan began to believe that anything was possible.

Evan has also kept his focus on school and has achieved awards there too, winning the 1999 Presidential Award for Academic Excellence. His goal after skating is to attend Harvard's business school and build a career in international business. In the meantime, skating is his priority — with a few time-outs to golf, go inline skating, listen to music or drive his car.

When it comes to sport, Evan doesn't believe in luck. He's based his success on hard training, the only thing that can give an athlete consistency and endurance. When he can count on that, even a less-than-perfect performance could send him home with another medal.

## Highlights

1st at Four Continents 2005

1st at Junior Grand Prix Final 2003

1st at Junior Olympics – Juvenile 1996

2nd at World Junior Championships 2004, 2003, 2001

3rd at World Championships 2005

3rd at Four Continents 2003

3rd at US Nationals 2005

# Cynthia Phaneuf

Born: January 16, 1988

In: Sorel, Quebec

Home: Contrecoeur, Quebec

Height: 167 cm (5'6")

Coaches: Annie Barabé, Sophie Richard

Trains in: Drummondville, Quebec

Choreographer: David Wilson

Category: Ladies' singles

Representing: Canada

No one was more shocked than Cynthia Phaneuf when she won the Canadian ladies' crown in 2004. It was just her second time as a senior national competitor, and to win the title she had to beat a strong and experienced field and dethrone the defending champion! At sixteen, it was a dream come true for Cynthia, who'd been skating since she was four.

Following her surprise triumph, a very tough decision had to be made. As senior champion, it was expected that she would represent Canada at the 2004 World Championships. But her coaches knew that, as a newcomer to the senior scene, Cynthia was not prepared to compete at the senior world level. A poor performance at such an important event could kill her motivation and self-esteem, two things her coaches were carefully building.

Instead of putting her into the biggest senior event, her coaches and Skate Canada decided to send Cynthia to the 2004 World Junior Championships, where she could gain some necessary international experience.

It proved to be the right move, one that gave Cynthia the confidence to carry the title of Canadian champion. In the fall of 2004, she competed at Skate America and Skate Canada, winning silver and gold respectively and qualifying for the Grand Prix Final.

But Mother Nature was about to intervene. Cynthia had a huge growth spurt, something that is very difficult for a skater's body to handle. Suddenly her muscles wouldn't respond as they used to and she lost most of her jumps . . . and with the jumps, most of her confidence too.

Now Cynthia is fighting back, but it's been a tough grind for someone who found success so quickly.

Even as a junior, Cynthia was known for her presentation and choreography. Her perfect posture, her costumes, her acting ability and her program details made her hard to beat at every level. Now that her growth has stabilized once again and her jumps have returned, watch as she continues her dream of capturing the skating world's biggest prizes.

## Highlights

1st at Canadian National Championships 2004

1st at Skate Canada 2004

2nd at Canadian National Championships 2005

2nd at Skate America 2004

2nd at Four Continents 2004

20th at World Championships 2005

# Evgeni Plushenko

Born: November 3, 1982

In: Solnechni, Russia

Home: St. Petersburg, Russia

Height: 178 cm (5'10")

Coach: Alexei Mishin

Trains in: St. Petersburg, Russia

Choreographers: Sergei Petukhov, Edvard Smirnov

Category: Men's singles

Representing: Russia

For a sickly child born to poor parents in Russia's far east, Evgeni Plushenko's rise to figure-skating stardom beat all the odds.

"Zhenya" (Evgeni's nickname in Russian) was only four when he inherited a pair of skates from a neighbor's daughter. With skating, his poor health began to improve. Encouraged by this, Evgeni's parents signed him up for more sports: skating, gymnastics, skiing, cycling — anything that would help him become stronger.

At first he was the smallest and youngest in his skating group, falling often and crying when other skaters made fun of him. But as he grew, Evgeni got tougher. He developed a talent for hard work and learned that by never giving up, his chances for success were greater.

Evgeni's first trainer was a former weightlifter, Mikhail Makoveyev, whose passion for skating was passed on to his young student. By seven Evgeni had won his first competition, and things looked rosy until 1993, when the rink in his home town closed to make way for a car repair shop.

He begged to be sent to St. Petersburg to train, but his family couldn't afford it. Finally Makoveyev stepped in and introduced Evgeni to a friend, someone who would be willing to take on this "diamond in the rough"— someone named Alexei Mishin.

Evgeni was only eleven when he moved away from home to train. Mishin, a coach of world champions, wasn't just taking on a new student, he was adopting a son, at times providing food and money, teaching Evgeni about life, making him part of the family.

In the following years, both skater and coach worked hard, Evgeni proving his technical brilliance with never-before-done quad-triple-triple combinations and Mishin designing the programs to showcase them. They've weathered many serious setbacks, most recently a tear in Evgeni's thigh muscle, an injury so painful he was forced to withdraw from the 2005 World Championships.

How does it affect his Olympic chances? With six Russian wins, four European championships and three world titles to Evgeni's credit, no one has better credentials to aim for Olympic gold.

And to think it all began on someone else's skates!

## Highlights

1st at World Championships 2004, 2003, 2001

1st at European Championships 2005, 2003, 2001, 2000

1st at Russian National Championships 2005, 2004, 2002, 2001, 2000, 1999

1st at Grand Prix Final 2005

2nd at Olympic Games 2002

# Shen ★ Zhao

Born: November 13, 1978 / September 22, 1973

In: Harbin, China

Home: Beijing, China

Height: 160 cm (5'3") / 177 cm (5'9½")

Coach: Bin Yao

Train in: Beijing, China

Choreographer: Lea Ann Miller

Category: Pairs

Representing: China

*I*t was 1996, in Edmonton, Alberta, when Xue Shen and Hongbo Zhao first caught the skating world's attention. The team hadn't been seen since the 1994 World Championships when they had finished twenty-first, mostly unnoticed.

In those two years, Xue and Hongbo had transformed from a stumbling pair of teenagers into well-trained world-class athletes. Their lifts and throws were gigantic, soaring above the ice. But they had no sense of music or body line, and apart from their huge lifts and jumps, the program was empty.

Bin Yao, their coach, could see that his team needed "packaging": good music, great choreography and a designer look. The quality of their skating he could handle; for the rest they needed outside help.

Yao and his students worked tirelessly with some of the sport's greatest experts. In the process, as things improved, the pair also discovered they had to learn to show emotion publicly, something that went against their cultural heritage.

Xue and Hongbo were born into simple working-class families. Xue's dad used to take her on his bike to the outdoor rink early every day to build up her stamina. At six, Hongbo was on a boys' basketball team.

When Yao, who was coaching in Harbin, saw how well Hongbo could move, he recommended skating instead.

The pair might never have gotten together if Hongbo's former partner hadn't retired. Xue was fourteen when she was asked to step in, something that excited and frightened her at the same time, since she was not as experienced as Hongbo.

On the way to becoming the first Chinese pair to win a world championship, Xue and Hongbo overcame many obstacles, but no challenge as great as the one they faced prior to the 2006 Olympic season. Hongbo tore his Achilles tendon and required emergency surgery, something doctors said could take five months to heal . . . with the Olympics only six months away. But Hongbo saw it as just one more obstacle to overcome along the pair's road to the Olympic title. As fans and experts know, counting this team out would be a big mistake.

## Highlights

1st at World Championships 2003, 2002

1st at Chinese National Championships 2002, 2001, 1999, 1998, 1997, 1996, 1994, 1993

1st at Four Continents 2003, 1999

2nd at World Championships 2004, 2000, 1999

2nd at Chinese National Championships 1995

2nd at Four Continents 2001

3rd at Olympic Games 2002

3rd at World Championships 2001

4th at World Championships 1998

5th at Olympic Games 1998

# Joannie Rochette

Born: January 13, 1986

In: Montreal, Quebec

Home: Ile Dupas, Quebec

Height: 157 cm (5'2")

Coaches: Manon Perron, Nathalie Martin

Trains in: St. Leonard, Quebec

Choreographer: David Wilson

Category: Ladies' singles

Representing: Canada

*F*ew skaters have accomplished so much in such a short time.

By the age of fifteen, Joannie Rochette had already won two back-to-back Canadian titles: the novice championship in 2000 and the junior championship just one year later.

Since then she has been on the senior national team, earning medals at every national event. In 2005 she finally added to her list of Canadian titles by winning the senior national championship.

Joannie started to learn to skate when she was three, in the small community of Ile Dupas. Her mother had put her in all kinds of sports, but skating was the one thing Joannie just kept on doing. As her skills improved, she eventually moved her training to St. Leonard on the island of Montreal.

When she isn't on the ice, Joannie spends her time studying natural and health sciences full-time at the Collège André-Grasset. She juggles ice time with class time, carving out a few special minutes to shop and go to the movies with friends.

Like many top-level competitors,

Joannie's skating success has come at some cost. In 2002 she suffered the whole season from shin splints so severe they kept her off the ice until only eight weeks before the 2003 Canadian Championships.

If there's been one jump that's proven difficult for Joannie to master, it's the triple Lutz. Her long-time coach, Manon Perron, recognized that Joannie was skating the jump incorrectly and insisted on taking it back to basics. After more than a year of hard work, Joannie finally found the proper technique, skating the Lutz cleanly in every part of the 2004 World Championships. In her free skate she nailed the Lutz along with five other triples to earn a 5.9 out of 6.0.

Joannie has always had superb jumping skills. Her exquisitely developing artistry, combined with those jumps, takes full advantage of recent changes in the scoring system. Thanks to choreographer David Wilson, she has also learned to paint a more mature and elegant picture on the ice — a picture that could feature an Olympic medal!

## Highlights

1st at Canadian National Championships 2005

1st at Trophée Eric Bompard 2004

2nd at Canadian National Championships 2004, 2003

3rd at Grand Prix Final 2004

8th at World Championships 2004

11th at World Championships 2005

# Emanuel Sandhu

Born: November 18, 1980
In: Toronto, Ontario
Home: Vancouver, British Columbia
Height: 183 cm (6')
Coach: Joanne McLeod
Trains in: Burnaby, British Columbia
Choreographer: Joanne McLeod
Category: Men's singles
Representing: Canada

Skating experts around the world consider Emanuel Sandhu one of the most talented athletes ever. He can do it all — eye-popping quadruple jumps, fast and original spins, and creative footwork. His choreography is generally considered some of the most artistic and musical ever presented on the ice.

Much of his superior style comes from his background as a student and performer with the National Ballet of Canada — he's been dancing on stage since he was three. Although Emanuel didn't start to skate until he was eight, it didn't take long for him to be noticed on the ice too.

Emanuel was in a group skating lesson at the local club near his home in Richmond Hill, Ontario, when a coach noticed that he "spotted" his spins, like a ballet dancer. That coach, Joanne McLeod, also noticed that he could land jumps cleanly and spin like a top — even though he was wearing skates two sizes too big.

Eventually the time came when Emanuel had to choose between the ballet studio and the rink. In the end, the soaring feeling that skating gave him won out, and McLeod found herself with a talented and challenging new student. Their bond has continued to grow — even when she moved her training site across the country to British Columbia, Emanuel followed, leaving his family behind in Ontario.

Ever since the moment when he burst onto the competitive scene back in 1998 by nearly upsetting the legendary Elvis Stojko at the Canadian championships, Emanuel has often been skating on thin ice. Despite winning three Canadian titles since then and receiving plenty of international applause, he's been bothered by an inability to skate cleanly at the world's biggest events.

Yet even with his roller-coaster performances — occasionally clean, but often not — Emanuel continues to excite and inspire audiences with his ability to interpret all kinds of music, from rap to pop to Prokofiev. Add to this his beautiful positions, the perfect stretch of his muscles and his elegance on the ice, and you've got the makings of a world champion.

## Highlights

1st at Canadian National Championships 2004, 2003, 2001

1st at Skate Canada 2004

1st at Grand Prix Final 2003

2nd at Four Continents 2004

7th at World Championships 2005

8th at World Championships 2004, 2003

# Fumie Suguri

Born: December 31, 1980
In: Chiba, Japan
Home: Yokohama City, Japan
Height: 157 cm (5'2")
Coach: Oleg Vasiliev
Trains in: Chicago, Illinois
Choreographer: Lori Nichol
Category: Ladies' singles
Representing: Japan

Fumie Suguri was born in Chiba, Japan, but spent several of her early years growing up in Alaska, where her father worked as an international pilot. With the long winters, it was natural for Fumie to try all sorts of winter sports. By the time she was six, and the family was moving back to Japan, she was showing signs of becoming a promising skater. At that point Fumie's mom did what every other mom would do — signed up her daughter at the local skating club.

These days Fumie laughs at the memory. If her family had only known how expensive it was to practise the sport in Japan, she likely wouldn't have continued, let alone become a two-time world bronze medalist and one of the world's best figure skaters!

To get there, Fumie has relied on funding from the Japanese Olympic Committee for some of her training expenses. But with circumstances becoming harder in Japan, ice rinks are closing down, forcing the country's many elite skaters to practise in crowded and therefore dangerous conditions.

For the four-time Japanese national champion, the situation was at a crisis point. Should she stay home where she was comfortable but where she couldn't train properly, or should she look at other training options?

It didn't take Fumie long to realize that if she wanted to improve, she was going to have to make major changes. She decided to go to North America to train. But where?

At the time, Fumie was scheduled to work on new programs with choreographer Lori Nichol, a Canadian. When Nichol went to Chicago to work alongside Russian coach Oleg Vasiliev, Fumie went too. She discovered that she loved the friendly atmosphere. Facilities were modern, the ice was good and she had room to move. She decided to unpack her skate bag and get to work.

Fumie has created a special style all her own. For her programs, she carefully chooses music that is rarely heard, allowing her to develop moves and steps that seem fresh and original.

With her new home training base near Chicago and plenty of ice time, Fumie is primed for her next Olympic battle. She knows what it's like to stand on the podium and hear the applause, and she's counting on her renewed enthusiasm to get her there again.

## Highlights

1st at Japanese National Championships 2003, 2002, 2001, 1997

1st at Four Continents 2005, 2003, 2001

1st at Grand Prix Final 2003

3rd at World Championships 2003, 2002

5th at Olympic Games 2005

# Totmianina ★ Marinin

Born: November 2, 1981 / March 23, 1977

In: Perm, Russia / Volgograd, Russia

Home: St. Petersburg

Height: 160 cm (5'3") / 187 cm (6'1½")

Coach: Oleg Vasiliev

Train in: Chicago, Illinois

Choreographer: Lori Nichol

Category: Pairs

Representing: Russia

When Tatiana Totmianina and Maxim Marinin won their second world pairs title in 2005 — an incredible feat for two athletes who never planned on skating pairs — it was the thirty-second time a Russian pair had won a world championship.

Tatiana and Maxim were singles skaters, both capable of triple jumps (including the triple Lutz) but facing hard competition in their solo events. Luckily they were realists too. Tatiana could see the high quality of the skaters she would have to face, and thought her chances for success might be better in pairs. Maxim made the decision to try pairs the day a gifted young upstart beat him.

In 1996 they teamed up. Although they had a rocky start learning all the lifts and moves, they found that their elegant style set them apart from other more acrobatic teams. Their individual jumping ability got them talked about too.

Their on-ice chemistry was harder to find. With little emotion or expression of the music, the team seemed destined for lower placements.

They wanted more, so in 2001 Tatiana and Maxim opted to leave Russia to train in the United States with Russian Olympic pairs champion Oleg Vasiliev. Living in Chicago and practising their English forced the couple to become more outgoing — something that showed in their skating when they became world champions in 2004.

Then disaster struck at a competition that fall. Tatiana was flying high in a lift when Maxim caught his edge and tripped, sending Tatiana crashing to the ice headfirst. Medical teams poured onto the ice to rush her to hospital and to console her shaken partner. In the end, Tatiana was lucky — her injuries limited to a concussion and bruises — and she was determined. Within weeks the team was back training, perfecting the same lift that could have ended their career.

Following the accident, the pair made several television appearances to talk about their frightening experience — something that helped to increase public awareness about the risks that can go along with competitive skating.

Did it frighten Tatiana and Maxim? Not enough to keep them from winning their second world title several months later, making them favorites to further Russia's gold history, this time at the 2006 Olympic Games.

## Highlights

1st at World Championships 2005, 2004

1st at European Championships 2005, 2004, 2003, 2002

1st at Russian National Championships 2005, 2004, 2003

2nd at World Championships 2003, 2002

4th at Olympic Games 2002

# Johnny Weir

Born: July 2, 1984
In: Coatesville, Pennsylvania
Home: Newark, Delaware
Height: 172 cm (5'8")
Coaches: Priscilla Hill, Tatiana Tarasova
Trains in: Newark, Delaware
Choreographers: Tatiana Tarasova, Evgeny Platov
Category: Men's singles
Representing: USA

As a twelve-year-old, Johnny Weir had visions of becoming a champion equestrian, not a champion skater. He was already an accomplished rider when he got interested in skating after watching it on TV.

Legend has it that Johnny's first time on the ice was behind his family's home, when the cornfield iced over and he tried skating between the frozen cornstalks. Soon he was taking lessons at the local rink and trying to do jumps on roller skates in his family's basement.

Then he was "discovered" and began serious private lessons. A few days a week, he would commute to Newark, Delaware, to work with former U.S. Ladies' competitor Priscilla Hill, still his coach today. The team clicked immediately. In fact, the magic was so strong that after only five years, Johnny won the world junior championship in 2001.

Knowing that Johnny's talent was special, Hill's challenge was in learning how to direct it without restricting him artistically, because seeing Johnny skate was more like watching ballet than skating — he looked as if he were floating.

As his devotion to skating grew, Johnny and his family moved to Delaware, where he could train full-time. He also enrolled at the University of Delaware as a linguistics and fashion design student. He enjoys designing his own costumes, trying to make them as unique as his own skating style.

Then came the 2003 U.S. Nationals and what Johnny calls the "Dallas Disaster." During his free skate, Johnny couldn't "find his legs" — a term skaters use for being off balance. After two nightmarish falls that sent him into the boards, he had to withdraw. The situation cost him his national ranking as well as the financial support that went with it.

Times were tough, but neither he nor his coach was about to give up. Instead they planned for his comeback with the toughest year of training in his life. The next year it all paid off. Not only did Johnny dethrone the defending national champion . . . he did it with a perfect mark.

Since then, he's repeated his national title and has come within an ice shaving of the World podium. If he can do that when everyone counted him out, taking on the world for an Olympic medal should be easy!

## Highlights

1st at US National Championships 2005, 2004

1st at NHK Trophy 2004

1st at Trophée Eric Bompard 2004

1st at Junior World Championships 2001

4th at World Championships 2005

5th at World Championships 2004

This book is dedicated to all the young people who read it, with the hope that the stories presented here will inspire you to follow your own dreams. No champion is "born" — champions win medals because they work hard, listen well, persevere and believe in themselves.
If they can do it, you can too!
Also, special thanks to Sandy and Diane. I dub you "Honorary Skaters"!
— *D.W.*

To all young skating fans, that you may find happiness in skating,
achieve your best and always dare to dream.
— *G.C.*

**Scholastic Canada Ltd.**
175 Hillmount Road, Markham, Ontario L6C 1Z7, Canada

**Scholastic Inc.**
557 Broadway, New York, NY 10012, USA

**Scholastic Australia Pty Limited**
PO Box 579, Gosford, NSW 2250, Australia

**Scholastic New Zealand Limited**
Private Bag 94407, Greenmount, Auckland, New Zealand

**Scholastic Ltd.**
Villiers House, Clarendon Avenue, Leamington Spa,
Warwickshire CV32 5PR, UK

Canadian ISBN 0-439-94704-9 / US ISBN 0-439-94612-3

**Library and Archives Canada Cataloguing in Publication**

Wilkes, Debbi
Skating superstars / Debbi Wilkes ; photographs by Gérard Châtaigneau.

ISBN 0-439-94704-9

1. Skaters —Pictorial works — Juvenile literature.
I. Châtaigneau, Gérard  II. Title.

GV850.A2W45 2005     j796.91'2'0922     C2005-905874-9

Text copyright © 2006 by Debbi Wilkes.
Photographs copyright © by Gérard Châtaigneau.
All rights reserved.

6  5  4  3  2  1     Printed in Canada     06  07  08  09  10